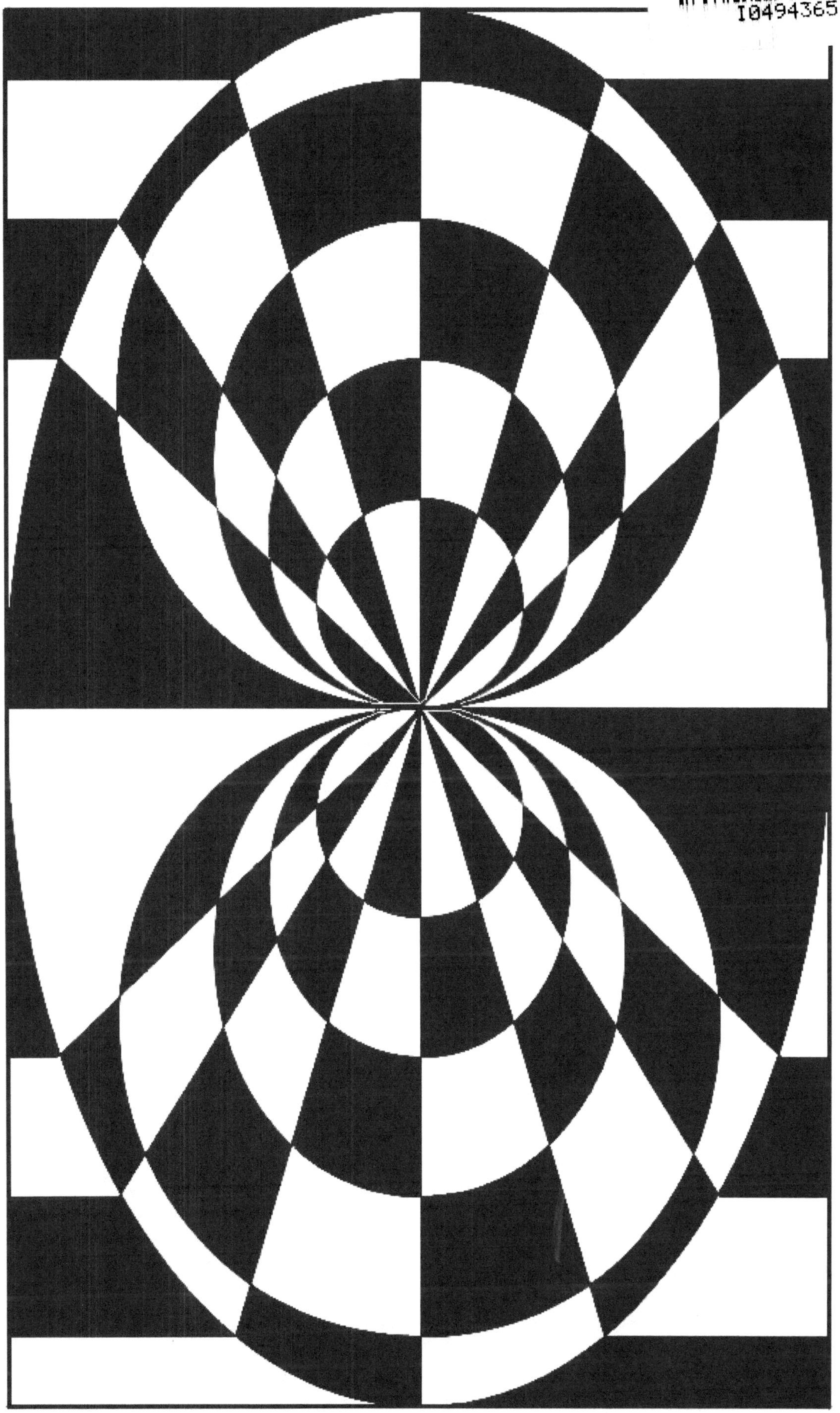

Visual Vertigo

Volume 2

Indies United Publishing House, LLC
P.O. Box 3071
Quincy, IL 62301-3071

www.indiesunited.net

BOOKS BY LISA ORBAN

OKAY, PICTURE THIS... SERIES
IT'LL FEEL BETTER WHEN IT QUITS HURTING
WINE COMES IN SIX-PACKS

I'D RATHER STARVE THAN COOK!
A cookbook for people who hate to cook.

ILLUSIONS BY LISA
Optical Illusions Coloring Book
Visual Vertigo Volume 1
Visual Vertigo Volume 2
Visual Vertigo Volume 3
Visual Vertigo Volume 4

Visual Vertigo

Coloring Book
Volume 2

Lisa M. Orban

Second Print Edition October 2018
Published by Indies United Publishing House, LLC

Copyright © December 2017 by Lisa M. Orban

All rights reserved worldwide.
No part of this publication may be replicated, redistributed, or given away in any form
without the prior written consent of the author/publisher or the terms relayed to you
herein.

First Print Edition December 2017

Cover art designed by Lisa M. Orban

Many thanks to author, RT Graham for your invaluable help in coming up with the
series title when I drew a complete blank...

...after drawing all the optical illusions.

ISBN-13: **978-1-64456-007-5**

The sale of this book without a cover is unauthorized.
If you purchased this book without a cover, the poor Indie author who slaved over a hot
computer to bring you this fine book did not receive any compensation for all of
her hard work and dedication. And just so you know,
every authorized book sale results in a happy dance by the author.
Please, be kind, and don't deprive the author of her happy dance just to save a few pennies.

To Cory

I really enjoyed watching
your eyes cross as I made these designs

If you enjoyed this coloring book, please consider leaving a review on GoodReads. You can use the QR Code below to take you directly there.

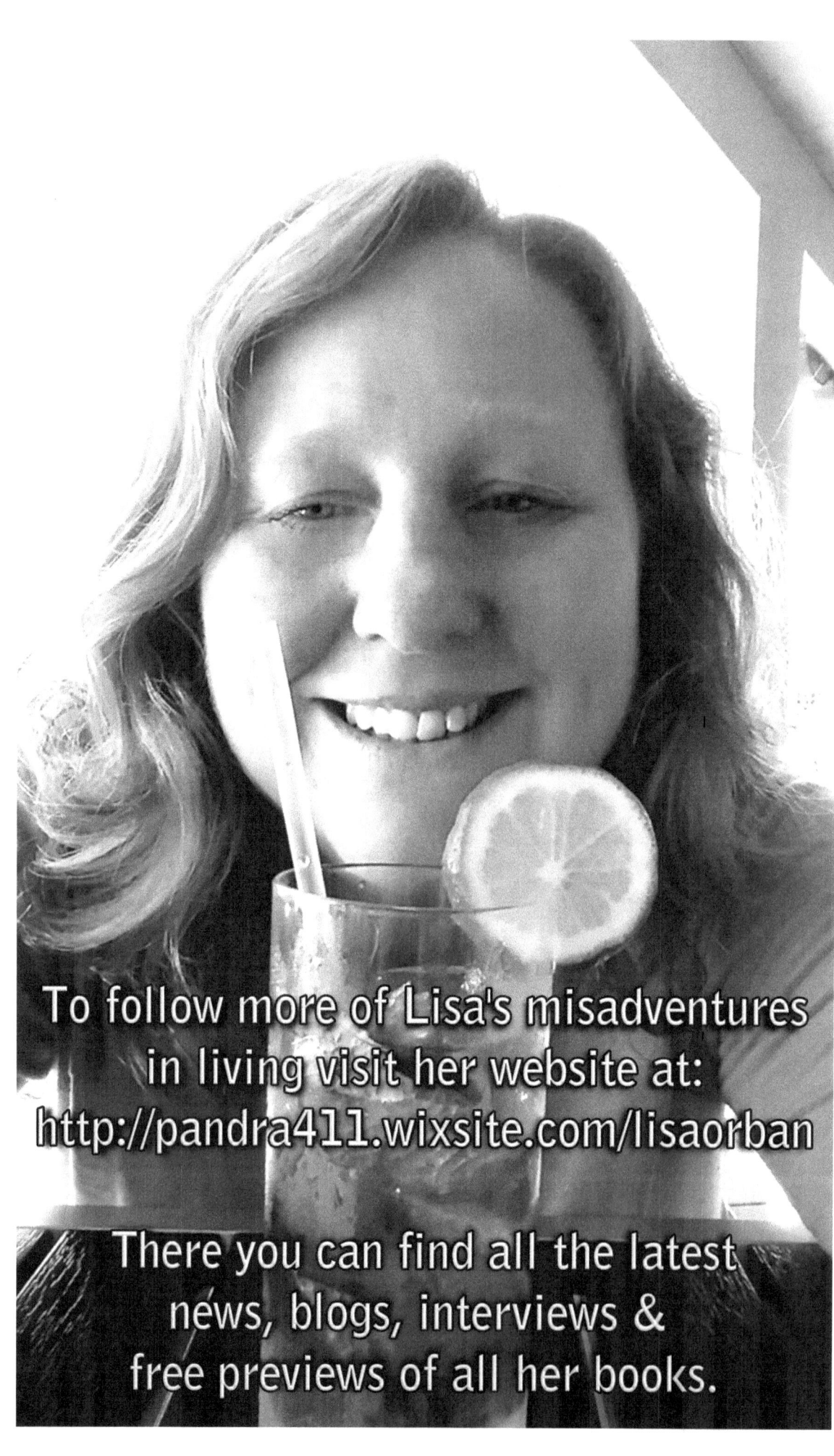

To follow more of Lisa's misadventures
in living visit her website at:
http://pandra411.wixsite.com/lisaorban

There you can find all the latest
news, blogs, interviews &
free previews of all her books.

www.ingramcontent.com/pod-product-compliance
Lightning Source LLC
Chambersburg PA
CBHW081242180526
45171CB00005B/518